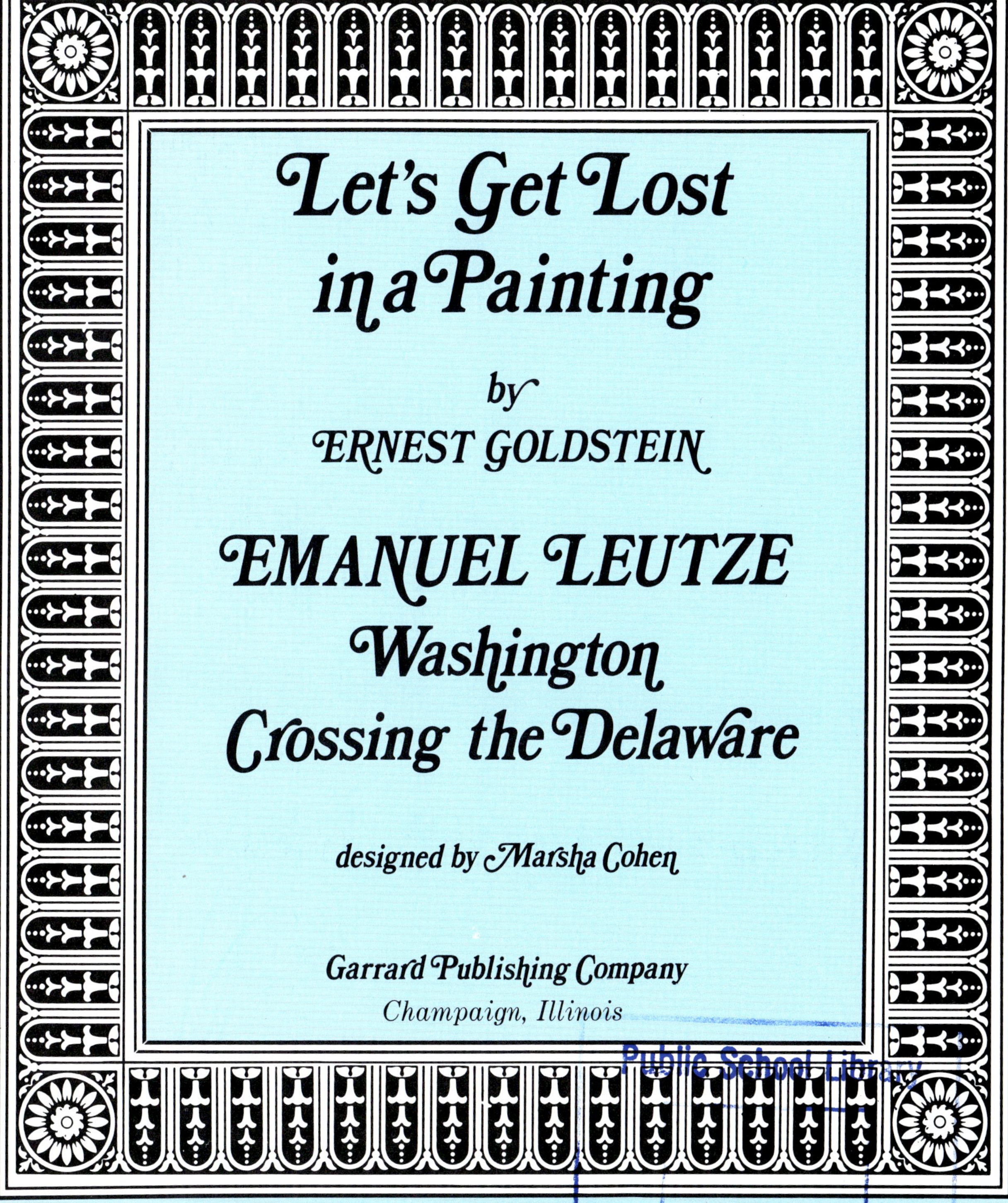

Let's Get Lost in a Painting

by

ERNEST GOLDSTEIN

EMANUEL LEUTZE
Washington Crossing the Delaware

designed by Marsha Cohen

Garrard Publishing Company
Champaign, Illinois

To
Ken and Jo

Diagram Concepts by Don Stacy

Drawings by Marsha Cohen
Robert Saunders, Series Consultant

Library of Congress Cataloging in Publication Data

Goldstein, Ernest, 1933-
Leutze, Washington crossing the Delaware.

(Let's get lost in a painting / Ernest Goldstein; 3)
Summary: Discusses historical, biographical, and artistic aspects of the well-known nineteenth-century painting.
1. Leutze, Emanuel, 1816-1868. Washington crossing the Delaware—Juvenile literature. [1. Leutze, Emanuel, 1816-1869. Washington crossing the Delaware. 2. Painting, American. 3. Art appreciation. 4. Washington, George, 1732-1799—Portraits. 5. United States—History—Revolution, 1775-1783] I. Title. II. Title: Washington crossing the Delaware. III. Series: Goldstein, Ernest, 1933- . Let's get lost in a painting; 3.
ND237.L6A76 1983 759.13 82-15403
ISBN 0-8116-1002-0

First Edition
Editorial and Production Services by Cobb/Dunlop, Inc.

Manufactured in the United States of America

Classic™ binding R.R. Donnelley and Sons Company
US patents pending

Photo Acknowledgments

Emanuel Leutze, *Washington Crossing the Delaware*, The Metropolitan Museum of Art, New York
Entire painting pages 4-5, 11, 13, 24, 27
Details pages 10, 12, 25, 39

John Trumbull, *Capture of the Hessians at Trenton, December 26, 1776*, Yale University Art Gallery
page 19

Thomas Sully, *The Passage of the Delaware*, Museum of Fine Arts, Boston
Entire painting page 20
Detail page 25

A Modern Recreation of the Crossing, Washington Crossing Foundation, Washington Crossing, Pennsylvania
page 22

George Caleb Bingham, *Washington Crossing the Delaware*, Chrysler Museum, Norfolk, Virginia
page 21

Jacques-Louis David, *Napoleon Bonaparte Crossing the Alps at the Great Saint Bernard Pass*, The Museum of Versailles, France
pages 29, 30

Charles Willson Peale, *Portrait of George Washington at Princeton*, Pennsylvania Academy of the Fine Arts
page 32

Gilbert Stuart, *Portrait of Washington (Vaughn)*, Metropolitan Museum of Art, New York
page 34

It is doubtful whether so small a number of men in so short a space of time had greater results upon the history of the world.

On the day before Christmas 1776, the Hessian commander in Trenton heard a startling rumor: George Washington was planning to cross the Delaware River and attack the British and Hessian troops. The commander, a certain Colonel Rall, roared with laughter. He is reported to have said, "If Washington and the Americans dare cross, I will personally chase them back in my stocking feet."

The colonel's statement tells much about the American army in the winter of 1776. The so-called army was a ragged group that had been defeated and driven from state to state and from river to river. The exhausted soldiers were suffering from lack of food, medical supplies, and protection from the cold. The winter had been especially severe—ice covered the Delaware River. Rall knew that that crossing was not only unthinkable, it was laughable.

On Christmas Eve, convinced that the rebellion would soon be over, Rall ordered his men to "lighten the guards and prepare for the holiday." This was Rall's last command. On the day after Christmas the American army had won the Battle of Trenton and the colonel was dead. He had made one fatal mistake. He and the entire British army had underestimated the character of a man and the power of an idea.

In 1851, 75 years later, an American artist living in Düsseldorf, Germany, finished painting his version of that fateful night. The public loved it immediately. To this day it remains America's most popular historical work, even though the artist is hardly known. The name of the painting is *Washington Crossing the Delaware*; the name of the almost forgotten artist, Emanuel Leutze (pronounced LOY-TSE).

You are about to take a journey into history through Leutze's painting. Since you have probably seen *Washington Crossing the Delaware,* stop before going on. Visualize the painting in your mind's eye. What do you remember most? Then go to the work. How much history can you read? What is the mood of the painting? Of the men in the boat?

What people see and remember most is a sublime George Washington. He is dressed in yellow knee breeches, high boots, a dark coat lined with yellow, a grey military cloak lined with red, and a black cocked hat. His sword hangs at his side and in his right hand he holds a spy glass. The confidence in his face and the quiet strength of his pose reassure the soldiers and tell of the coming victory. But the power of his look goes beyond that one battle. He is the commander-in-chief who has measured the shoreline and the statesmen already planning the future of the young country.

A critic praised this picture because "unlike many good historical paintings which must be studied before being appreciated, Leutze's immediately strikes the eye." What you notice first is Washington. His stance and stature give a feeling of calm and control. But the artist has created an illusion. Once you go beyond the standing figure the mood quickly changes to extreme danger. Wind, currents, and ice threaten the boat. The men battle the river, the cold, and their own fatigue. Hidden beneath Washington's gaze is turmoil, commotion, and great physical tension. Look at the arrangement of the men in the boat. What is each man doing?

While the men appear to be in control, they are actually struggling. Study their various positions. Each body turns in a different direction. Each turn represents a human force against the force of the elements. Each twist of a body creates more tension and more activity. With such turmoil, why, asked one critic, is Washington standing? Before going on, look at the positions of the men again and try to answer this question.

Let's imagine Leutze's problem: how to dramatize the history of the country with a few men in a small boat. The men are not posing for a picture. Every action in-

Figure 1 pushing ice floes
Figure 2 pushing ice floes
Figure 3 rowing
Figure 4 watching for danger
Figure 5 flagbearer
Figure 6 flagbearer
Figure 7 rowing
Figure 8 huntsman holding a gun
Figure 9 watching for danger
Figure 10 awaiting the battle
Figure 11 helmsman using an oar as a rudder

creases the feeling of danger outside the boat and the commotion within. In the drawing (page 8) the figures have been turned into cube-like forms. Without the soft textures of their clothing, it is easier to follow the variety of ways Leutze positioned the bodies. The cubes allow you to feel the activity. In this presentation every action becomes an essential part of the final design.

Notice how the angled bodies of the men create a circular motion around the fixed stance of Washington. He is the axis within the moving circle. As the men work together around him, his position stabilizes the boat.

Inside the small area of a boat, Leutze made a compact design. He succeeded in creating tension and movement from eleven men working furiously, cramped and huddled together. The term for this technique in art is "depth of motion." Leutze then calms the swirling motion with the standing figure. The arrangement of men dramatizes danger, while Washington's fixed position makes order out of chaos.

The dangers outside the boat can be seen in the sea of ice. The artist designed the ice floes as heavy floating shapes of death—wandering aimlessly with the currents, banging against the boat. The drawing below shows the complex details of the two main ice floes.

Only a small portion of the ice floes shows above the water, like icebergs, most is hidden below. So it is hard to judge their real size. Imagine they are above the water, then they could easily be as large as the boat. These giant floes are like mountains with jagged rocks jutting out in all directions. In the drawing, the threat of these pointed shapes can be felt. On the lower right ice chunk, Leutze's name is splattered in blood. The two large ice floes in the foreground take on the shapes of frozen masks of death floating in the water. The response to the threat is the calm look of Washington, repeated in the flagbearers, the huntsman, and in the helmsman at the rudder.

Nature's shapes are terrifying and destructive. Without Washington's presence the boat could end up like the large tree twisted into the ice.

Leutze resolves the conflict by the stability of the boat. It seems to be going smoothly ahead. But this is another

illusion. The boat is rocking but the design hides the movement.

The drawing shows the directions of the oars and the flag. Each oar slants in a different direction. By slanting them at various angles, Leutze shows the force of wind and currents. These diagonal lines break the circular motion and create another visual movement. The six major lines (the five oars and the flag) together with the soft curves and the other slanted lines in the drawing give the impression of a rocking boat. The lines move to the rhythm of the currents in the water.

It may be difficult to visualize this rocking motion because the oars are arranged in triangular shapes. To Washington's right the two oars meet to form a triangle.

To his left another triangle is made up of the huntsman's gun and the oar.

Notice the constant repetition of triangular shapes within the boat: the left leg of figure 1, Washington's left arm and right leg, the body position of figure 4 (see page 7).

If you extend the angles of the front and rear oars they meet to form a large pyramid at the top of the boat.

The triangles and the large pyramid give a feeling of stability. The boat rests on the water in the same way a stepladder stands on the ground. The ladder balances when the two equal opposite forces meet to form the apex of a triangle. At the center of this large pyramid the artist braced his "ladder" with another triangle: a "V" made by the line of Washington's head and back against the flag.

The "V" is the artist's final touch. It takes two men to hold the flag. As the wind whips against the flag it is met and balanced by the force of Washington. The final design gives the feeling and creates the illusion of balance, stability, and calm.

The danger in the painting and the harshness of the elements accurately depict what Washington and his men faced during the winter of 1776—the most desperate moment of the American Revolution. Washington had planned to cross the river and attack in early evening. The Americans were to cross in three groups: the first under his command; the second under the command of General Cadwalader; and the third under General Ewing. But the crossing was so difficult that Cadwalader and Ewing had to turn back. It was not until four o'clock on the morning of the next day, December 26th, that Washington's forces reached the New Jersey shore, ready for the nine-mile march to Trenton.

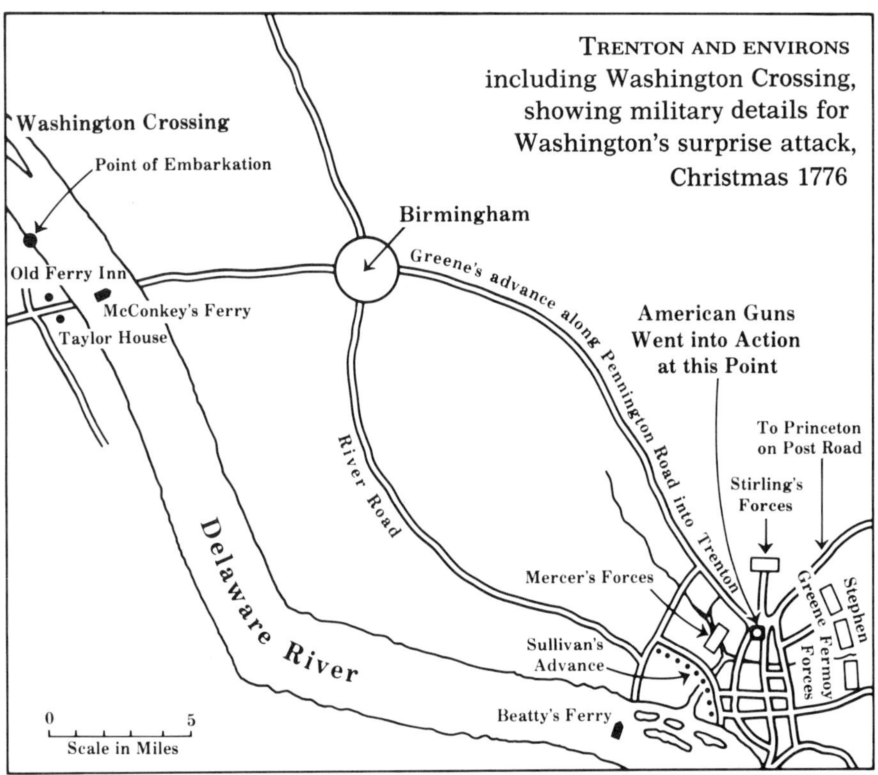

Only Washington's will got the men across. The men, already exhausted, were beginning to freeze. So pitiful was their condition that a messenger who followed them tracked their route easily "by the blood on the snow from the feet of the men who wore broken shoes."

One hour after daylight on December 26th they arrived in Trenton. The Hessians, totally surprised, at first fought but then surrendered. After the battle, Washington reported the victory to Congress: approximately 80 Hessians killed, 900 others captured with a large store of supplies and ammunition. The Americans lost four men —two killed in the fighting, two others frozen to death during the crossing.

The victory at Trenton changed the course of the American Revolution. The inexperienced volunteers who had fled in terror from the Hessian bayonets had finally beaten their dreaded enemy. It was a victory not measured by the number of men killed or captured. It was the beginning of an army fighting for a cause that was not hopeless. Coming after a long series of defeats it gave fresh courage to the cause of freedom. Years afterward the English writer A. G. Trevelyan described the importance of Trenton:

> "It is doubtful whether so small a
> number of men in so short a space
> of time had greater results upon
> the history of the world."

Seventy-five years later, Emanuel Leutze put a small number of men in a boat and painted his version of *Washington Crossing the Delaware.* Leutze was born in Germany in 1816. When he was nine his family came to America. The young Leutze grew up in Philadelphia, and probably visited the place where Washington made the crossing. While still in his teens, he showed such artistic talent that he was sent back to Europe to complete his art studies. In 1849, in his studio in Düsseldorf, Germany, he began to work on *Washington Crossing the Delaware.* He finished the painting in 1851, then came back to America where he remained until his death in 1868. During the two years of painting the *Crossing* there were several interruptions, including a fire which partially destroyed the first canvas. Upon its completion, Leutze sent the painting to New York for exhibit and the public loved it immediately. In time the work became popular around the world. Just a few years ago when representatives from The People's Republic of China came to the Metropolitan Museum of Art in New York City, the one painting they knew and recognized was *Washington Crossing the Delaware.*

And yet, as popular as the work is, almost no one knows Leutze's name. In a strange way the popularity of the painting has worked against the artist; the work has been taken for granted. Historians look for errors, artists neglect it, and writers often omit this work from art books. Yet the painting continues to please new generations. It remains *the* popular image of the crossing. This, by itself, is interesting since Trenton had long stirred the imagination of artists. On the following pages you will look at versions of the crossing by three of America's foremost artists: John Trumbull, Thomas Sully and George Caleb Bingham.

John Trumbull had been a soldier in the Continental army. In 1794 he painted *Capture of the Hessians at Trenton.* Under a large wind-swept sky the Hessians surrender to Washington. In the background an American flag rises in the breeze while in the front the Hessian banner lies on the ground. The ceremony is formal; the battle is over. Trumbull was the "patriot painter" of the American Revolution. His work celebrates the men who fought. The key identifies every major figure in his picture. (page 18-19)

In 1819 Thomas Sully received a commission to paint *The Passage of the Delaware* for the capitol building of

1. **Edward Wigglesworth** 1742-1826 Merchant and sea captain of Newburyport, Massachusetts; Revolutionary soldier; member of the Massachusetts General Court; Collector of the Customs at Newburyport.
2. **William Shepard** 1737-1817 Of Westfield, Massachusetts; Revolutionary soldier; member of Congress.
3. **Josiah Parker** 1751-1810 Of "Macclesfield," Isle of Wight County, Virginia; Revolutionary soldier; member of Congress.
4. **James Monroe** 1758-1831 Of "Oak Hill," Loudon County, Virginia; President of the United States; Revolutionary soldier, statesman.
5. **Johann Gottlieb Rall** 1720-1776 Colonel of Hessians serving with the British during the Revolution; killed at the Battle of Trenton; (posthumous portrait).
6. **William Stephens Smith** 1755-1816 Lawyer of New York, and Lebanon, New York; Revolutionary soldier; Secretary of Legation, London; member of Congress.
7. **Robert Hanson Harrison** 1745-1790 Lawyer of Charles County, Maryland and Alexandria, Virginia; Revolutionary soldier; Chief Judge of the General Court of Maryland; (from memory).
8. **Tench Tilghman** 1744-1786 Of Maryland and Pennsylvania; Revolutionary soldier; volunteer aide-de-camp and secretary to Washington by whom he was chosen to carry to the Continental Congress the news of the Surrender of Lord Cornwallis.

Capture of Hessians at Trenton, December 26th, 1776 by John Trumbull

9. **George Washington** 1732-1799 LL.D. 1781. Of "Mt. Vernon," Virginia; first President of the United States.
10. **John Sullivan** 1740-1795 Lawyer of Durham, New Hampshire; Revolutionary soldier; member of Congress; Governor of New Hampshire.
11. **Nathanael Greene** 1742-1786 Of Rhode Island and "Mulberry Grove," Savannah, Georgia; Revolutionary soldier; Quartermaster General.
12. **Henry Knox** 1750-1806 Of Boston, Massachusetts and "Montpelier," Thomaston, Maine; Revolutionary soldier; Secretary of War.
13. **Philemon Dickinson** 1739-1809 Lawyer of New Jersey and Pennsylvania; Revolutionary soldier; United States Senator.
14. **John Glover** 1732-1797 Of Marblehead, Massachusetts; Revolutionary soldier often in charge of transportation; secured boats for the crossing of the Delaware.
15. **George Weedon** *c.* 1730-1793 Innkeeper of Alexandria, Virginia; Revolutionary soldier.
16. **William Washington** 1752-1810 Planter of Virginia and "Sandy Hill," St. Paul's Parish. South Carolina; Revolutionary soldier, cousin of General Washington.

The Passage of the Delaware by Thomas Sully

North Carolina. But the painting was too large for the wall space and was rejected (12' X 17'). This splendid work now hangs in the Museum of Fine Arts in Boston. Sully depicts Washington and his men preparing to cross the river. He is mounted on a white horse atop a snow-covered hill and is watching men in uniforms at the left pushing a cannon while boatloads of troops cross the river below.

George Caleb Bingham's *Washington Crossing the Delaware,* completed in 1871, has a dramatic and beautiful mood. In front of a blue dawn-lit sky, a thoughtful Washington is seated on a white horse. His gaze is di-

Washington Crossing the Delaware by George Caleb Bingham

rected toward the shore. The crossing has been made and the boat is ready to land.

The works of Trumbull, Sully, and Bingham are important and each can be studied and appreciated on its own terms. Thomas Sully's painting had been the most popular in America. Leutze's work not only replaced it but made Sully's *Passage* obscure. These three paintings are just as good as Leutze's (in the opinion of many they are better). But only Leutze's work is seen everywhere—in schools, libraries, books and even in other paintings.

All of the artists took certain liberties with historical truth. The characters in Trumbull's work might or

A modern re-creation of the crossing in a Durham boat. Washington Crossing, Pennsylvania.

might not have been at Trenton. In Bingham's painting you will find to the left of Washington another famous American who was certainly not at Trenton, Andrew Jackson. Bingham, a Midwestern artist who painted life on the Mississippi River, took other liberties in his painting. His Washington resembles a riverboat man who appears in his other paintings, and the boat is a Mississippi river raft.

The boats used in the crossing were the Durhams. These boats hauled cargo between New Jersey and Pennsylvania. (Washington had the Durham boats available because he had deliberately taken them during his initial retreat across the Delaware.) They were long, low boats and held between 30 and 40 people.

Leutze did not have a model of the Durham boat, nor would it have suited his purpose. His boat with the twelve figures permits the viewer to see each individual effort as part of the overall design.

Leutze's work does not have the sweep of a Trumbull sky, the beautiful harmony of color and movement of Sully's masterpiece, nor Bingham's quiet mood of dawn on the river. But it has something that immediately strikes the eye. It has action and courage. The other paintings are quiet, almost subdued by beauty. Leutze's work is full of passion. It has drama! It portrays courage. It tells the story of that supreme moment when one man changed the course of history. It is the missing page of the book. It is a country's history in a small scene. In an action-packed, condensed area it tells everything about the conditions and the man.

All the works are historical paintings, but Leutze's has one important difference. Traditional historic paintings celebrate great events with large panoramas in which the eye wanders over the entire canvas. Go back and look at these three works. The vast sweeps of land and sky require time and study. They take our attention away from the central figure. In all of the paintings Washington is the center, but only in Leutze's work does all the action focus directly on him.

Although his *Crossing* is a history painting, the dramatic events lead to a historical portrait. The tension, the battle against the elements, the fears of the men, and the future of the country are all resolved in this heroic portrait. It is the portrait of a man; it is also a portrayal of that moment when the fate of the country hung in the balance. Leutze shows that particular moment depicting the condition of the army in the clothes of the men, the distance of the boat from the shore and the time of day

(or night). Look at the painting again. What does the dress of the men tell you? Who are they? Who can you identify?

When the painting was first exhibited, Leutze wrote a short description for the catalog: "The picture reproduces the moment when the great general is steering to the opposite shore in a small boat surrounded by eleven heroic figures — officers, farmers, soldiers, and boatmen." Leutze could not possibly have painted their actual clothes. But he had made a life-long study of the Revolution. The clothes on Leutze's figures follow Washington's own descriptions of the Continental army before the crossing. They did not have uniforms because they were not yet an army. The soldiers were exhausted, their condition weak. The man with the bandage around his head recalls Washington's report of their condition: seven out of every ten men were sick, wounded, or unable to fight. *If Rall were watching he might have laughed!*

The only figures to be positively identified are the officer supporting the flag, young Colonel James Monroe (later President Monroe), and the black man at the oars to Washington's right who is Prince Whipple. Prince Whipple also appears in Sully's painting at the right of Washington.

Prince Whipple's place in the pictures at a time when slavery existed in America is an important statement. Whipple's personal story is also a fascinating piece of Americana. According to historical records he was born in Africa of fairly wealthy parents. At about the age of ten he was sent to America to be educated—"to enjoy the benefits of the New World." On the way, a treacherous ship captain brought him to Baltimore where he was sold as a slave. The man who bought him was General Whipple of New Hampshire. During the Revolution he was given his freedom and served first under General Whipple and later under Washington. It is not clear whether Sully or Leutze knew the incredible story of blacks who chose to come to America, but Prince Whipple's place in their paintings tells much about both artists' vision of America.

The location of the boat in the water tells us the time (hour) of the picture. Can you determine how far the boat is from shore? How long have they been on the water? Look at the painting, then go to the diagram.

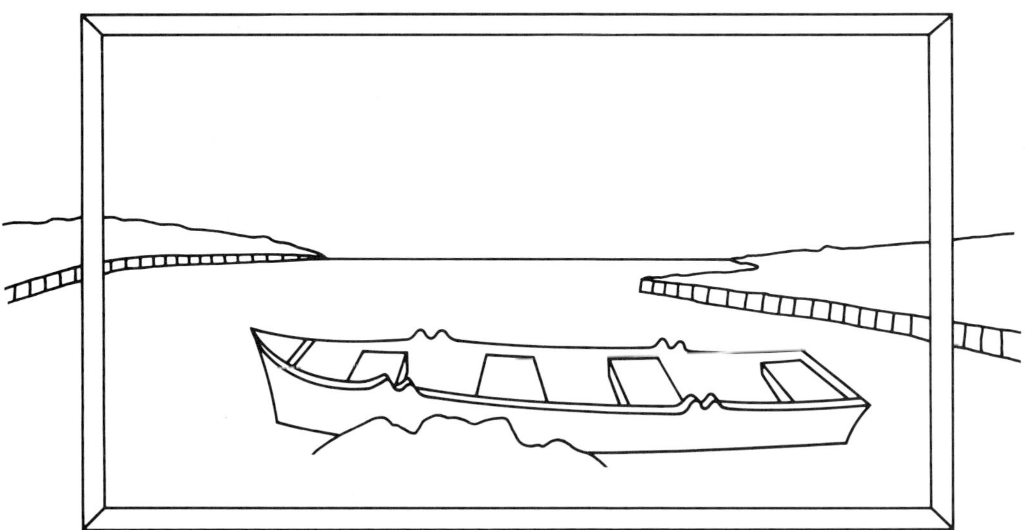

The diagram shows the boat without the men. You can get an idea of the boat's location by finding both shorelines at the back corners of the picture. On the left side is the New Jersey shore. If you follow the long line of boats behind Washington you come to the other shoreline. When you extend the shorelines outside the picture frame you realize that the boat is actually quite far from both shores, somewhere in the middle of the river. It looks close, but this is another illusion. Since they left in late afternoon on the 25th and did not arrive until the next morning (December 26th), they have been on the water for several hours.

From the artist's use of light, can you determine the time of day (or night)? Out of the dark night haze the line of boats leads up to the front. In the sky shines the last star of night—the morning star. The boat is moving toward the light of dawn. Washington is standing in the center of the light; the effect is theatrical—as if Leutze had thrown a spotlight on him. You can see his use of light in a black and white version of the painting.

In the black and white version you get the feeling of a drama. The dark haze above has the shape of a theater curtain. On stage the spotlight falls on the boat. Since the eye seeks and follows light, the white (or light) leads the eye from right to left. The light pushes the boat from the densely packed (dark) right into the open lighter area to the left. The boat moves in the same direction as the gaze of the standing figure in the center of the light.

Washington's placement at center stage has another theatrical effect. Leutze has raised him above the men. His position suggests a rider on a horse. He has mounted the boat and is riding out the storm.

The position recalls a dangerous crossing from another world-famous painting: *Napoleon Bonaparte Crossing the Alps at the Great Saint Bernard Pass* by the French artist Jacques-Louis David. If you get to Versailles and see this work you will note just how much one artist influences another. Washington's breeches are the same yellow as those of Napoleon.

David painted the work in 1804, four years after Napoleon had crossed the Alps during his Second Italian Campaign. The crossing of the Alps was dramatic and dangerous. In the background the army moves slowly over the ice. In the foreground Napoleon is mounted on a spirited horse. Like the mood in Leutze's work, the action is violent but the picture is calm. Notice how carefully David fixes Napoleon's leg on the horse and turns his calm and determined face to the viewer. The position of the horse rearing up almost out of control is an illusion. It is no match for the power and control of the rider. Notice the triangular shape of the left leg firm in the stirrup and the left hand clenching the reins. The position balances the wild movements of the animal. As the right arm points the way, you can read David's vision of

Napoleon Bonaparte Crossing the Alps at the Great Saint Bernard Pass
by Jacques-Louis David

Napoleon. The face of Napoleon carries greatness and calm and dominates the picture.

Although Washington is standing and Napoleon sitting, their positions are remarkably alike.

Compare Washington's stance with Napoleon's position on his horse. In both pictures the exaggerated triangular shapes of legs and arms anchor the actions and keep the eyes locked on the face.

David was a close friend of Napoleon and his portraits are the result of their time together. Leutze worked many years after the death of Washington. Since photography had not been invented in Washington's time Leutze had to work from portraits of other artists.

There was no shortage of portraits. America after the Revolution was in the age of portrait painting. The heroes of the war were the subjects of the artists. And the man they celebrated most was George Washington. Artists came from all over America and Europe to paint his portrait. The quickest way to a fortune was a successful portrait of Washington. Once you have seen several of the portraits it is apparent that no two are alike. It would be impossible to study them and determine the exact likeness of the man.

Washington's family considered Charles Willson Peale's *George Washington at Princeton* to be the truest portrait (page 32).

The victory at Princeton came soon after Trenton. Peale had been a soldier with Washington and was a close friend of the family. The painting shows Washington at ease, resting an arm on a cannon. Peale painted this portrait in 1779 at the request of the Supreme Executive Council of Pennsylvania. It was to be an official state portrait. Official portraits are usually formal and "stiff," but here you can feel the warmth of Washington in his relaxed pose. His face, full of pride and confidence, reflects the victories at Trenton and Princeton. In the left background, American soldiers are leading British prisoners to the buildings at Princeton College. To the right above Washington, an American flag with the thirteen stars of the colonies unfurls over the fallen Hessian banners. This picture had something special to tell Leutze. Historians critical of Leutze have noted that Congress had not yet approved the American flag at the time of Trenton. Peale had been at Trenton and is highly re-

George Washington at Princeton by Charles Willson Peale

garded for his accuracy. He had studied the exact military details of the battle. The American flag in his picture proves that a flag had been established at Trenton.

The enormous range in the portraits reveals the different qualities of Washington's greatness. Some artists painted him as a general, others as a statesman, and still others as a successful businessman. The two most important portraits, however, were inspired by Washington the horse trader. One is by Gilbert Stuart; the other by the French sculptor Jean-Antoine Houdon.

Gilbert Stuart is considered America's foremost portrait painter. Because of his reputation, Stuart was able to get Washington to sit three different times. The result was three different paintings. During the first two portraits relations between artist and subject were formal and cold. Stuart was a brilliant talker and could excite people with his conversation. During the first sitting as he chatted on subjects he thought important to the President, Washington remained silent. Stuart complained that the instant Washington started to sit he became totally distant, almost bored. The result is the first portrait —known today as the Vaughn Portrait (page 34).

When the portrait was first shown it was highly praised, and many experts still consider it the best. But Stuart felt it was a failure—and Peale agreed. When Peale saw it he said "if some day in the future Washington returned to life and should stand side by side with this portrait, he would be rejected as an impostor."

The second time the sittings were even stormier. By then Stuart was angry. He hated to dress his subjects in fancy lace or place them in elegant settings in full portrait—the very things he put into the second portrait, the Landsdowne portrait (page 35).

Portrait of Washington by Gilbert Stuart
THE VAUGHN PORTRAIT

Portrait of Washington by Gilbert Stuart
THE LANDSDOWNE PORTRAIT

This full-length portrait shows Washington holding a sword, with his right arm extended in a theatrical pose. But Stuart noticed something else. Washington was having trouble with his newly made teeth. His lower plate fitted him so badly that it pulled the lower part of his face out of shape. Look closely at the mouth in the Landsdowne portrait. The jaw takes away the heroic effect. Washington looks like he is clenching his teeth and his eyes, half closed, are distant. By Stuart's time George Washington had become a legend all over the world. We can only guess what Stuart had in mind, but this is not the presentation of the legend. Perhaps it is Stuart's reaction to the Washington who took no pleasure in his gossip and chatter. Stuart's second portrait is of a man who still remained distant and cold to him.

In 1796 Stuart did his third portrait of Washington at Mrs. Washington's request. Stuart's studio in Philadelphia was an old stone barn. When Washington first appeared Stuart noted that his false teeth had been fixed. Stuart started to talk and again Washington did not relax. Suddenly Stuart looked up and saw a gleam in his eye and a smile flash across his face. Stuart was amazed. Washington had seen a splendid horse gallop by the window and immediately the face became alive. Stuart started to talk about a local race horse. From horses the conversation went to farming; again Washington's face became alive and spirited. As Washington talked Stuart worked. The result of that one moment is the sum of a lifetime, the Athenaeum portrait!

Everything about the man Washington is captured in this work. It is a picture of dignity, thought and assurance. There are no props; the head stands out all by itself. Light falls on the face and reveals a strong jaw, thought-

Portrait of Washington by Gilbert Stuart
THE ATHENAEUM PORTRAIT →

ful eyes, and a firm mouth. Many Americans know only this portrait of Washington because it appears on the dollar bill. Others think that to know this one is enough.

Leutze had been impressed by Stuart's Athenaeum portrait. In preparation for his own work he had made several studies of it. To this day there are copies of the Athenaeum portrait in museums signed "artist unknowned." The unknown artist is Emanuel Leutze. But when it was time to select the model for his painting, Leutze went to the work of the French sculptor Jean-Antoine Houdon.

Houdon had left France for Mount Vernon in 1785 to make a bust for a statue of Washington. During the sitting Houdon was having a difficult time. Washington's face had the gloomy stare he saved for these occasions. Suddenly an unexpected arrival interrupted. A man, a horse trader, was brash enough to insult Washington's knowedge of horses. Washington's face lit up and the sculptor put his expression in the clay bust. By a stroke of luck, Houdon succeeded.

Since Washington was considered to be the greatest horseman of his time, both these stories could be true. It is certainly of interest to note that the best portraits of Washington were not inspired by war, politics or business but by his love of horses and his knowledge of farming.

The Athenaeum portrait and the Houdon bust are both important works, but the Houdon bust was Leutze's choice for his Washington. Leutze owned a rare copy of a mask made from the bust and is thought to have made a special trip to America to get it. Go to the Houdon mask. What does it tell about Leutze?

This French artist, the greatest sculptor of his age, had something special to tell about the universal quality of

Mask of Washington by Jean-Antoine Houdon
(The Leutze-Stillwagen Mask)

George Washington. The mask kept the faithful likeness of the man but the noble face has a sublime expression. It is slightly uplifted and looks to the future. His gaze goes beyond time and space. That expression is the exact look Leutze wanted at the top of the pyramid of his storm-tossed boat.

Why would Leutze do such a painting 75 years after Trenton? And why this particular scene when it had already been painted by so many other artists? Perhaps we will never know why and how an artist chooses his subject, but the history of Leutze's life provides a clue. In his catalog description of the painting, Leutze hoped it "would have a special meaning for these troubled times." The year 1849 when Leutze began this work was a period of turmoil in Europe. Germany was a confederation of small states governed by feudal lords and princes. In 1848 there had been a revolution that tried to unite the country and bring freedom to the people. It failed and Germany went through a period of chaos and repression. The failure of the revolution was a devastating blow to Emanuel Leutze. By then he had become a world-famous artist. Almost all of his paintings celebrated scenes of human liberty. A typical example of his earlier work is the founding of America in *Columbus Returning in Triumph to Queen Isabella* (1843).

It is easy to see the difference between *Columbus* and *Washington Crossing the Delaware. Columbus* is a traditional historic painting with far less power, design, and intensity than *Crossing the Delaware.* But the times had changed. The year 1849 was a desperate moment in the life of the artist. His response to the failure of the 1848 Revolution was a painting so huge that it takes up an entire wall of the Metropolitan Museum of Art. It is 14 feet high and 20 feet wide. You approach it looking up in the same way you look up at a monument. It is a monument in painting. It has the size, grandeur and simplicity necessary for a monument; simplicity meaning the story "immediately strikes the eye." The boat serves as the wide base of the monument. The arrangement of

Columbus Returning in Triumph to Queen Isabella (1843)

men makes Washington larger than life. There he is, seated on a horse in public view.

The reason why Leutze chose a crossing for his most important work has its roots far back in time. For ages the crossing of a river has been one of the most powerful images of meeting and fulfilling destiny. The Bible tells of Joshua's "one more river to cross" when he tamed the mighty waters of the Jordan and lead his people to the promised land. The Greeks had to cross the River Styx to their final destination. Caesar faced his moment of truth when he crossed the Rubicon. In her book on Emanuel Leutze, *Portrait of Patriotism*, Ann Hutton wrote "every man as well as every nation makes just such a crossing once in a lifetime." The moment for Leutze's crossing was 1849. Through that one work, different from anything he had done, Leutze made his commitment to freedom in a monument to George Washington.

History explains why Leutze chose the Washington of Houdon instead of David's Napoleon. The American Revolution fired the shot heard 'round the world. It was Washington who sparked the later revolutions for freedom in Europe. Napoleon Bonaparte had brought war to Europe in the name of freedom. But after his victories he proclaimed himself emperor. During the nineteenth century the image of Napoleon declined, while George Washington—the man who spurned a throne—became a universal symbol of human liberty, the very essence of the Houdon bust. That bust portrays grandeur. His look goes beyond time and place to link this one artist's agony to his hope for mankind.

History provides still one more reason for the standing figure. Because Leutze worked 75 years after Trenton, the painting represents his view of Washington's place in America. The different positions around the central figure, pushing in all directions, could be the competing interests of the young country. After the Revolution, America was threatened by the conflict between the states. Many historians claim that if Washington had not become President the union might not have survived. From those early conflicts Washington's vision of America emerged. A few years after the French Revolution, Britain and France were at war and feelings in this country ran high. Thomas Jefferson, mindful of the debt to France, wanted to help the French. Alexander Hamilton wanted to help the British. Between these two towered the position of George Washington. He said it makes no difference who wins in Europe—the United States must be a haven of liberty for all. History proved him right.

Washington was more than a general. In Leutze's vision he was all that was noblest and best in the American people. As men made fortunes from war, he even refused his salary as general. With no thoughts of himself, he assumed every responsibility put upon him and fulfilled it. But his image as the greatest horseman of his time, the inspiration of Stuart and Houdon, lingers on in the *Crossing of the Delaware.* When Leutze stood him up and mounted him on a boat, he sent him on a journey through time with his message to the world: *Freedom is the only king.*

This message has spoken to generations ever since. Almost one hundred years later at Iwo Jima, in one of the bloodiest battles of World War II, American soldiers were struggling to plant the flag. That moment was captured by a photographer and later in a sculpture at the Marine Memorial in Arlington, Virginia. The diagonal line of the flag and the grouping of the soldiers into the frozen drama come right out of *Washington Crossing the Delaware* (page 44).

There is still no answer to an impossible question raised earlier in this book: Which is the better painting — Leutze's, Sully's, Trumbull's or Bingham's? The fact remains that this one work of the German immigrant has become the American symbol for courage and triumph. When he packed the nation's history onto his canvas, he put us all into the boat under the determined gaze of the standing figure. His look into the future is a country's bond with its past. Leutze's Washington is the heart

The Marine Memorial in Arlington, Virginia

and soul of America. Since the business of art is to bring us closer to life, his painting brings us closer to the best part of ourselves through the man who was the best of his time, perhaps of all time.